W9-AUU-188

Dinosaurios y animales prehistóricos/ Dinosaurs and Prehistoric Animals

Tigre dientes de sable/Sabertooth Cat

por/by Helen Frost

Traducción/Translation: Dr. Martín Luis Guzmán Ferrer

Editor Consultor/Consulting Editor: Dra. Gail Saunders-Smith

Consultor/Consultant: Jack Horner, Curator of Paleontology
Museum of the Rockies
Bozeman, Montana

Capstone
press

Mankato, Minnesota

FREEPORT MEMORIAL LIBRARY

3 1489 00551 4177

Pebble Plus is published by Capstone Press,
151 Good Counsel Drive, P.O. Box 669, Mankato, Minnesota 56002.
www.capstonepress.com

Copyright © 2007 by Capstone Press. All rights reserved.
No part of this publication may be reproduced in whole or in part, or stored in a retrieval system, or
transmitted in any form or by any means, electronic, mechanical, photocopying, recording, or otherwise,
without written permission of the publisher. For information regarding permission, write to Capstone Press,
151 Good Counsel Drive, P.O. Box 669, Dept. R, Mankato, Minnesota 56002.
Printed in the United States of America

1 2 3 4 5 6 11 10 09 08 07 06

Library of Congress Cataloging-in-Publication Data
Frost, Helen, 1949–
    [Sabertooth. Spanish & English]
    Tigre dientes de sable = Sabertooth cat/de/by Helen Frost.
    p. cm.—(Pebble Plus. Dinosaurios y animales prehistóricos = Pebble Plus. Dinosaurs and
prehistoric animals)
    Includes index.
    ISBN-13: 978-0-7368-6685-9 (hardcover)
    ISBN-10: 0-7368-6685-X (hardcover)
    1. Smilodon—Juvenile literature. I. Title: Sabertooth cat. II. Title. III. Pebble Plus. Dinosaurios y
animales prehistóricos.
QE882.C15F7618 2007
569'.74—dc22
                                             2005037477

Summary: Simple text and illustrations present sabertooth cats, their body parts, and behavior—in both
    English and Spanish.

Editorial Credits
Martha E. H. Rustad, editor; Katy Kudela, bilingual editor; Eida del Risco, Spanish copy editor; Linda Clavel,
    set designer; Jon Hughes, illustrator; Wanda Winch, photo researcher; Scott Thoms, photo editor

Photo Credit
Folio Inc./Richard Cummins, 20–21

The author thanks the children's library staff at the Allen County Public Library in Fort Wayne, Indiana,
for research assistance.

Note to Parents and Teachers

The Dinosaurios y animales prehistóricos/Dinosaurs and Prehistoric Animals set
supports national science standards related to the evolution of life. This book describes
sabertooth cats in both English and Spanish. The images support early readers in
understanding the text. The repetition of words and phrases helps early readers learn
new words. This book also introduces early readers to subject-specific vocabulary words,
which are defined in the Glossary section. Early readers may need assistance to read
some words and to use the Table of Contents, Glossary, Internet Sites, and Index sections
of the book.

Table of Contents

Tabla de contenidos

A Prehistoric Mammal

Sabertooth cats were
prehistoric mammals.
Sabertooth cats lived more
than 1 million years ago.

Un mamífero prehistórico

Los tigres dientes de sable eran
mamíferos prehistóricos. Los tigres
dientes de sable vivieron hace más
de 1 millón de años.

Sabertooth cats lived
in grasslands and forests.

Los tigres dientes de sable vivían
en las praderas y los bosques.

How Sabertooth Cats Looked

Sabertooth cats were about the size of a lion. They were about 3 feet (1 meter) tall.

Cómo eran los tigres dientes de sable

Los tigres dientes de sable eran como del tamaño de un león. Medían cerca de 1 metro (3 pies) de alto.

Sabertooth cats had
two long, sharp teeth.
They had strong jaws.

Los tigres dientes de sable tenían
dos dientes alargados y afilados.
Sus mandíbulas eran muy fuertes.

Sabertooth cats had
short, strong legs.
They could run fast
across grasslands.

Los tigres dientes de sable
tenían las patas cortas y
fuertes. Podían correr muy
rápido por las praderas.

13

What Sabertooth Cats Did

Sabertooth cats hunted
and ate other animals.
They killed their prey
with their sharp teeth.

Qué hacían los tigres dientes de sable

Los tigres dientes de sable
cazaban y se comían a otros
animales. Mataban a sus presas
con sus afilados dientes.

Sabertooth cats opened
their mouths wider than
other animals. This helped
them swallow prey.

Los tigres dientes de sable podían
abrir su boca más que los otros
animales. Esto los ayudaba a
tragarse a su presa.

Sabertooth cats
may have lived
in groups.

Los tigres dientes
de sable vivían
en grupos.

The End of Sabertooth Cats

Sabertooth cats died out

about 10,000 years ago.

No one knows why they all died.

You can see sabertooth cat fossils

in museums.

El fin del tigre dientes de sable

Los tigres dientes de sable desaparecieron

hace cerca de 10,000 años. Nadie sabe

por qué murieron todos. Se pueden ver

fósiles de tigres dientes de sable en

los museos.

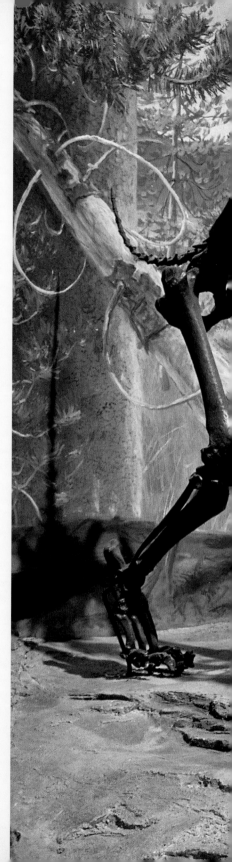

Glossary

fossil—the remains or traces of an animal or a plant, preserved as rock

grassland—a large, open area where grass and low plants grow

hunt—to chase and kill animals for food; sabertooth cats hunted and ate other animals.

mammal—a warm-blooded animal with a backbone; female mammals feed milk to their young.

museum—a place where objects of art, history, or science are shown

prehistoric—very, very old; prehistoric means belonging to a time before history was written down; dinosaurs and woolly mammoths are prehistoric animals.

prey—an animal that is hunted for food

Glosario

cazar—perseguir y matar animales para comérselos; los tigres dientes de sable cazaban y se comían a otros animales.

el fósil—restos o vestigios de un animal o una planta que se conservan como piedras

el mamífero—animal de sangre caliente con columna vertebral; las hembras de los mamíferos alimentan a sus crías con leche.

el museo—lugar donde se exhiben objetos de arte, historia o ciencias

la pradera—superficie grande y abierta donde crecen hierbas y plantas bajas

prehistórico—muy, muy viejo; prehistórico quiere decir perteneciente a una época antes de que hubiera historia escrita; los dinosaurios y los mamuts lanudos son otros animales prehistóricos.

la presa—animal que se caza para comerse

Internet Sites

FactHound offers a safe, fun way to find Internet sites related to this book. All of the sites on FactHound have been researched by our staff.

Here's how:

1. Visit *www.facthound.com*

2. Choose your grade level.

3. Type in this book ID **073686685X** for age-appropriate sites. You may also browse subjects by clicking on letters, or by clicking on pictures and words.

4. Click on the **Fetch It** button.

FactHound will fetch the best sites for you!

Index

Sitios de Internet

FactHound proporciona una manera divertida y segura de encontrar sitios de Internet relacionados con este libro. Nuestro personal ha investigado todos los sitios de FactHound. Es posible que los sitios no estén en español.

Se hace así:

1. Visita *www.facthound.com*

2. Elige tu grado escolar.

3. Introduce este código especial **073686685X** para ver sitios apropiados según tu edad, o usa una palabra relacionada con este libro para hacer una búsqueda general.

4. Haz clic en el botón **Fetch It**.

¡FactHound buscará los mejores sitios para ti!

Índice

FREEPORT MEMORIAL LIBRARY

0 1100 00001 1170

$10.00

FREEPORT MEMORIAL LIBRARY
FREEPORT, NEW YORK
PHONE: 379-3274

FREEPORT MEMORIAL LIBRARY
CHILDREN'S ROOM   GAYLORD M